The smallest Sheepdog

Written and illustrated by Cait Stott

Josie hope you enjoy the book, love Cait :)

This is Floss, she is the Mam of five beautiful puppies. Mac is the smallest puppy. He has one brother and three sisters.

When the pups reached eight weeks old it was time for them to leave the farm. One by one, Mac's brother and sisters went to live with their forever families.

Weeks and months went by, but no one came for Mac.
After some time, Floss had to return to working with
the sheep. Mac was sad and all alone.

One day, Mac was feeling brave and he decided to explore the farm. While exploring he made friends with a cat named Scruffy.

Mac and Scruffy spent their time laughing and playing. Their favourite thing to do together was to chase the field mice.

After watching Mac and Scruffy play together, Farmer Scott decided that Mac would become the farm's next sheepdog in training.

On the first day of sheepdog training,
Farmer Scott quickly discovered Mac was afraid of sheep!
"It's ok, you can do it Mac!" Shouted Farmer Scott,
just as two large sheep stomped towards Mac.

"Help!" Woofed Mac, as he fled across the field away from the scary sheep.

Mac ran across the farm to find Scruffy.
"I'll never be a good sheepdog," he whimpered. "Sheep are just too big and scary!"
"Don't be silly Mac" Scruffy meowed back.

"If you picture them as woolly jumpers with legs, then they're not so scary. Remember you are the one in charge, they have to listen to you, and you have to show them who's boss!"

Mac later returned to his training, remembering what Scruffy had said. He took a deep breath and thought to himself, "I am in charge, I can do this!"

Mac tried his very best, and eventually, he got better and better at working with the sheep. The more he practised, the less scary they became.

Mac put in lots of hard work, completing months and months of training.

Now Mac was confident working with the sheep. Farmer Scott decided that Mac was finally ready for his first ever sheepdog trial.

"Good luck in your competition!" Meowed Scruffy. "I knew you could do it, you will make a great sheepdog."

"Thank you!" Mac woofed back.
"I will do my best."

It was time for Mac to get ready for the competition. Farmer Scott gave Mac a bath and brushed his fur, making sure he was nice and clean.

After Mac's bath, it was time to set off.
Mac was feeling excited.

Mac and Farmer Scott arrived after a long drive.
Mac was starting to feel nervous.

British Sheepdog Society

He thought back to the day when he first began his training and said to himself "I'm so glad I didn't give up!"

Eventually it was Mac's turn to run, and luckily his hard work paid off. Mac finished one point ahead and was the overall winner in his class.

"Well done Mac, you did it!" Shouted Farmer Scott. As Mac sat proudly on the podium with his bright red first place ribbon.

There are 16 bunny rabbits hidden throughout the book, did you spot them all?